Index

Acknowledgments

The publishers would like to thank the following for their assistance in supplying equipment and materials for the book:

Alan Holtham, Cheshire

Axminster Power Tool Centre, Axminster, Devon

Crown Hand Tools Ltd, Sheffield, Yorkshire

Elu Power Tools Ltd, Slough, Berkshire

Foxell & James Ltd, London

J Crispins & Son, London

JSM Joinery, London

Morgans of Strood, Strood, Kent

Parry Tyzack, London

Peter Child, Essex

Racal Health & Safety Ltd, Greenford, Middlesex

Wilson Bros., Northfleet, Kent

The publishers and photographers would like to thar the contributors for their patient help and advice. Sp thanks go to Mark Ripley for his skills and imaginatic and clear demonstrations of techniques. Thanks also the following for their help on location shoots: Gord Stone, Paul Mitchard, Graham Mills, Gurk, Darren Fr; John Ingram, John Taylor and Mick O'Donnell.

All photography by Colin Bowling and Paul Forrester Hamlyn.

Editorial Manager: Jane Birch

Senior Designer: Claire Harvey

Project Manager: Jo Lethaby

Designer: Mark Stevens

Picture Researcher: Christine Junemann

Senior Production Controller: Louise Hall

Sanders and finishers

Belt sander
A sander capable of removing a great deal of material very quickly.

Random orbital sander
A sanding machine that does not leave scuff marks in the finished work.

Spindle sander
An oscillating spindle sander used for sanding small curved components.

Disc sander
A useful machine for trimming and shaping end grain and shaped or curved components.

Orbital sander
A flat half-sheet sander that has been largely superseded by the random orbital sander.

Detail sander
Used for sanding into small awkward corners.

Disc sander and finisher
Useful for general shaping and sanding components.

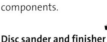

Belt cleaner
Abrasive cleaning stick – prolongs the life of sanding belts and discs by removing clogging deposits.

Hammers and screwdrivers

Pin hammer
Very popular hammer, used for all pinning and light work.

Cross-peen hammer
Known as a cross peen or joiner's hammer, used for driving nails.

Carpenter's mallet
Used for driving a chisel through a job.

Claw hammer
The most common carpenter's or joiner's hammer, used for driving nails and designed with a claw for removing nails.

Ratchet screwdriver
Drives screws by pumping the handle in and out.

Club hammer
Another useful tool for assembling furniture, used to apply the shock to drive glue out of the joint.

White rubber mallet
Useful for assembling furniture.

Cabinet screwdriver
So-called because widely used by cabinetmakers for driving screws.

Awls
Two patterns of awl here: the bradawl, with a smooth circular blade, and the birdcage awl with a four-sided blade. The latter is most useful for positioning screws when hinging.

Introduction

WORKING WITH WOOD, one of the most beautiful and versatile materials known to man, is a truly satisfying pastime. It is a challenge that leaves a tangible trail of the woodworker's progress from early mistakes to fine achievements, which can take the form of furniture and other well-designed and useful items. An important part of progress in the craft involves learning to make the various joints by hand. This rewarding process instills a sensitivity and understanding that will not be lost even if machinery is later introduced into the workshop.

The first section of *Joints and Jointmaking* provides comprehensive coverage of the basic joints used in woodworking, allowing you to undertake with confidence the four projects described in the second section of the book. Here, there are lists of materials and tools, plans and full instructions for undertaking the projects – a table, a mirror frame, a sturdy

bookcase and a tray – each of which relies on a specific jointmaking technique.

Lastly, the book includes a directory of the hand and small machine tools most commonly found in the small workshop. So, get yourself a good basic tool kit, familiarize yourself with the tools and how to look after them, and have a go! You will be amazed at how quickly your woodworking skills will improve and just how much satisfaction you will gain from your achievements.

Above *A typical home workshop showing a range of benches, and tools stored on walls and shelves*

Left *It is a joy to work with hand tools on a good sturdy work-bench; this one has an enviable Scandinavian vise system*

Woodworking joints

THE FOLLOWING PAGES illustrate a series of basic joints and simplify all the steps involved. Once mastered, knowledge of these joints will enable you to work competently with wood and construct items for yourself. It is advisable to practice the joint concerned before moving on to a specific project. It is worth remembering, too, that hardwoods are easier to work with than softwoods for quality joinery and are recommended for both practice and projects alike.

Lap joints

THE LAP, OR HALVING, JOINT is a basic joint with little structural integrity. It depends on glue for strength and may be reinforced with screws or nails. The shoulders of the joint do, however, impart rigidity to frame work. For work requiring intersecting frame members , the cross-lap joint is the only option.

The most common use of the lap joint is in softwood joinery and construction work where it is used with nails or screws. The joint works best in straight-grained wood, which allows the waste to be chopped out quickly and accurately. Straight grain is also important for strength. Since the joint removes half of the thickness of the stock, the remaining wood must be free of defects or short grain if the strength of the frame is not to be compromised.

For making any joint it is important to follow through the sequence on both parts of the joint

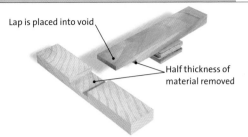

Lap is placed into void

Half thickness of material removed

LAP OR T-SHAPED HALVING JOINT *Lap joints are used to join two members of the same thickness by removing half of the thickness of each, and placing them together so as to fill the void in each.*

at the same time, that is, mark out both parts of the joint, cut all the shoulders, and so on. This way, if you are making several joints, the work proceeds in a consistent way. You will get into the rhythm of each operation, and the job will be both quicker and more accurate.

Making a T-lap joint

TOOLS & EQUIPMENT

Pencil and try square

Marking or cutting gauge

C-clamp

Tenon saw

Marking knife

Chisel

Smoothing plane

Glue and brush

USEFUL ALTERNATIVES OR EXTRAS

Frame miter saw with depth stop, band saw or radial arm saw with dado head for cutting shoulders

Router for removing waste

MARKING OUT

1 Using a sharp pencil and a try square, mark two lines across the first component the width of the piece of wood that is to be let into it.

2 Mark a line around the end of the second piece. The distance marked from the end of this piece is equal to the width of the first piece.

Ensure that the handle of the square is held firmly against the wood so that the blade is perpendicular to the work. Remembering to work from the face side and face edge, use the square to mark the line on the two edges.

Possible variations of the basic joint

Corner and cross-lap joints are developments of the T-shaped lap joint. In the case of the corner lap joint, both parts of the joint are identical.

The process for the cross-lap joint uses the same marking technique as for the first part of the T-shaped lap joint shown in Step 1 (opposite), but this time on both pieces of wood.

3 Set the marking gauge to half the thickness of the board. Check this on a piece of scrap stock of the same thickness by marking from each side.

4 Mark the sides of the joint on both parts. Shade the parts to be removed. (Note: some woodworkers may prefer to use a cutting gauge.)

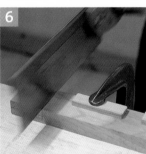

CUTTING THE SHOULDERS

5 To cut the joint, first secure the work firmly by C-clamping it to the worktop. On the first component cut the shoulders of the joint using a tenon saw. You can make a start for this cut by scoring a line with a marking knife and carefully chiseling a "V." However, with a bit of practice this may become unnecessary.

6 Repeat this process with the other piece of the joint. On the second component saw the shoulder at the end.

REMOVING THE WASTE

7 After making the crosscuts, use a sharp chisel to remove the waste, using a series of shallow cuts. Waste from a lap joint on

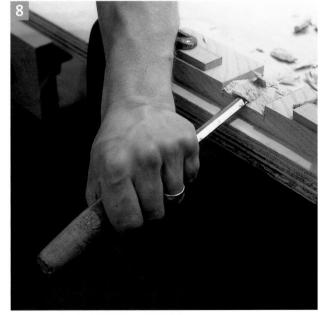

the end of a rail may be removed either with or across the grain.

Start from one side and begin cutting about ¹⁄₁₆ inch (2 mm) from the top of the wood, with the chisel pointing up slightly.

8 Return to the first component and repeat this process until, in small increments, you reach the gauged line. This line acts as a guide for the chisel on the final cut. Turn the work around and repeat the process.

9 When complete, there will be a slight hump in the cheek of the joint which may now be pared off level using the chisel. (Alternatively, remove the waste by sawing or using a router.)

ASSEMBLY

10 Fit the two parts of the joint together. Some fine planing may be required to ensure a snug fit.

Before gluing, prepare two small squares of scrap – hardboard or something similar – to protect the work from the C-clamp.

Apply glue evenly to all of the meeting faces using a small brush (it can be helpful to have one piece of wood clamped to the bench, the joint overhanging), and gently clamp.

When the clamp is on and some pressure has been applied, check that the shoulders are fully together and finally tighten the clamp.

When the glue is almost dry, pare off the surplus with a chisel. This is a lot neater than wiping it off while it is still wet.

Above *A basic T-shaped lap joint, ready for assembly*

Dowel joints and biscuit joints

THE DOWEL JOINT is a simple extension of the butt joint. In the butt joint, two flat edges or faces are simply glued together with no integral structure. In the dowel joint, dowels – short round pegs, normally made of beech but sometimes metal or plastic – are fitted in the joint and contribute both structural strength and additional gluing area.

The dowel may be used in any frame or carcass joint that is not likely to be subjected to heavy stress. In such situations, the speed and simplicity of the dowel make it an attractive alternative to stronger, more complex joints.

Biscuit joints are a development of dowel joints (see page 15).

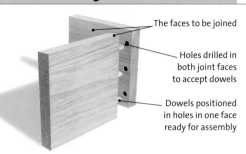

The faces to be joined

Holes drilled in both joint faces to accept dowels

Dowels positioned in holes in one face ready for assembly

Dowel joint *The dowel joint is a means of joining components in similar situations to mortise and tenons, tongue and groove and dovetails, but using dowels – short wooden pegs – to attach the two joint faces. Biscuits can be used in place of dowels to achieve a similar result.*

Making a dowel joint

TOOLS & EQUIPMENT

Marking or cutting gauge

Try square and pencil

Drill press or electric drill on stand

Lip-and-spur dowelling bit (with depth stop or masking tape)

C-clamps

Piece of plywood, approximately) 3–4 inches (75–100 mm) wide x ¼inch (6 mm) thick

Panel nails and hammer

Glue and brush

Countersink (drill) bit

Masking tape

Mallet

USEFUL ALTERNATIVES OR EXTRAS

Ready-made doweling jig

Center finder to help mark holes

MARKING OUT

1 The aim in marking out dowels is to produce rows of corresponding center marks on two different pieces of wood. The face and the edge of the joint are marked in exactly the same way.

Set a marking gauge to half the thickness of the stock; run it along the end of the face part of the joint to make a centerline.

1

2 Mark the intervals of the dowels across the center line using a small try square. The space between the dowels varies according to the size of dowel and type of work. For a ⁵⁄₁₆-inch (8-mm) dowel the spacing may be 1 inch (25 mm) in frame work and 3–4 inches (75–100 mm) in edge joints.

Measure and mark the intervals on the face part of the joint only. Extend the pencil marks right to the end of the workpiece.

3 Scribe the intervals on the corresponding part of the marked piece.

4 Next, run the marking gauge along the face of the end grain part of the joint to produce a centerline.

Possible variations of the basic joint
Both dowel and biscuit joints are highly adaptable and can be used easily in situations where other joints may be awkward, for example where angles other than 90° are involved. They also provide a viable alternative to the dado joint (see page 26).

5 Continue the scribed marks across the end grain of the piece using the small try square.

This marking method is applicable when the holes are to be bored freehand. However, if more than one or two joints are to be made, it is quicker and more accurate to make a jig (see Figure 10). Instead of using the marking gauge and pencil for marking the dowel centers, you could use an awl or a center punch to make a precise hole at the cross point of the lines to ensure that the center lip of the drill bit will locate in the correct position.

6 If you are not using a jig, now drill the sets of holes in each joint face, positioning the drill accurately and using a depth stop (see Figure 9). First drill the holes marked on the face side of

the wood, securing the work on the bench with a C-clamp.

7 Insert the other piece in the bench vise and drill the holes in the end grain.

MAKING A JIG FOR BORING

8 A doweling jig has two functions: it removes the need for a lot of time-consuming marking out and it guides the drill bit, increasing accuracy. You can buy one ready-made but it is easy to make one yourself in the workshop, as here.

You should make the jig from a rectangular section of wood, the same thickness as the stock being used and the same overall length as the dowel joint that is being made.

Mark out the narrow edge of this section in the same way as a dowel joint with a centerline and marks indicating the hole centers. Any inaccuracies in the jig will be transferred to the whole job, so it is essential to take care at this stage.

The boring is best done with a bench drill or an electric drill on a stand. This will produce a clean, straight hole and, in turn, better joints. Bore the holes for the jig with the same bit that is to be used for the dowels.

9 Tight-fitting rubber stops are available for lip-and-spur dowel boring bits. These are rings that slide up to the required position on the bit and indicate when the correct depth has been reached. This depth is equal to the depth of the jig plus half the length of the dowel plus $\frac{1}{16}$-inch clearance. (A little masking tape wrapped around the bit makes an alternative depth marker.)

10 Pin and glue a piece of plywood the same length as the jig, 3–4 inches (75–100 mm) wide and ¼ inch (6 mm) thick, to the side of the jig. This plywood piece forms a clamping bracket for fixing the template to the work.

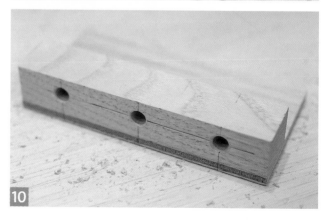

USING THE JIG

11 Lay the face side part of the joint on the bench with the joint projecting over the edge of the bench and clamp it, leaving the joint area free of obstruction. Align the ends of the jig with the ends of the work. Fix the jig to the work with panel nails through the plywood or small C-clamps across the jig itself.

Double-check the depth stop against the work (see Figure 9). Hold the drill steady while boring: to prevent damage to the jig, do not start the drill until the bit is in the guide hole.

Next, transfer the jig to the end-grain part of the joint. The set-up is the same except that the jig is mounted at the end of the workpiece. The annual rings in the wood cause the density to vary across the width of the board and a firm grip on the drill is required to prevent the drill bit from wandering.

12 Once drilled, either from the marking out or the jig, slightly countersink the holes – this aids alignment and accommodates any dust or excess glue.

Sticking tape up to the edge of each joint makes applying the glue easier and aids cleaning up later. Apply glue to both parts of the joint, the holes and dowels. Tap the joint together and clamp until dry.

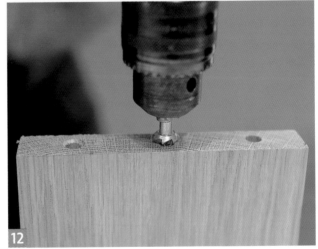

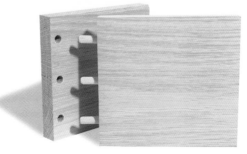

Above *A half-assembled dowel joint*

Making a biscuit joint

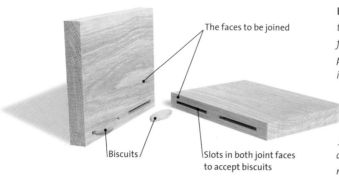

The faces to be joined

Biscuits

Slots in both joint faces
to accept biscuits

Biscuit joint *The joint is similar
to the dowel joint, but relies on
flat oval-shaped pieces of compressed beech called "biscuits,"
instead of dowels, glued in slots
"sawed" in components.
Moisture from the glue
causes the biscuits to expand,
forming a strong joint. The slots
are made with a portable
machine called a biscuit joiner.*

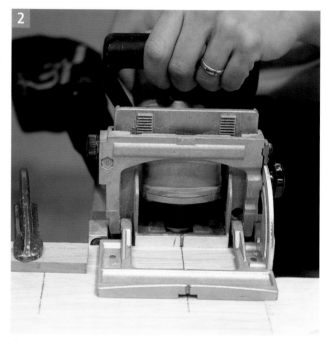

1 Marking out biscuit joints is simpler than marking dowels as the base plate of the biscuit joiner has preset center and end alignment marks. The slots need be only every 6 inches (150 mm), and are marked with a short perpendicular line.

2 Hold the fence of the joiner against the face of the work and align the center of the base with the marked line. Plunge to the preset depth. For butt jointing repeat the process on the edge of the corresponding piece. For right-angle jointing, position the fence against the edge of the corresponding piece and plunge the jointer to a preset depth into the face of the work.

Gluing and assembling a biscuit joint is just as for the dowel joint (see page 14). The biscuit is made of compressed wood and much of the strength of the joint is derived from the fact that the grain direction of the biscuit is diagonal and from the way that it swells with the moisture of the glue applied in the slot.

Mortise-and-tenon joints

THE MORTISE AND TENON is a strong joint used primarily in frame construction, although it can also be applied to carcass work. The mortise is the female part of the joint; the tenon is a rectangular piece that fits inside it.

Since it is so strong, the mortise and tenon provides the ideal solution when making frames that are liable to be used under stress. In table frames, for example, the main alternative are dowels, which are unlikely to stand the test of time. Good-quality door frames are usually mortise and tenoned and the joint is used extensively in production joinery.

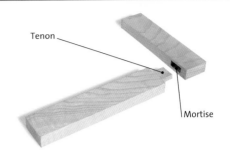

Mortise-and-tenon joint *This joint comprises a rectangular hole in the edge of one component, called a mortise. The projecting tenon, on the end of the other component fits the mortise precisely.*

Making a mortise-and-tenon joint

TOOLS & EQUIPMENT

Try square, pencil and metal rule

Mortise and marking gauges

Bench dogs or C-clamps

Mortise chisel and mallet

Masking tape

Tenon saw

Bevel-edged chisel

Smoothing plane

Glue and brush

Sash clamp

Abrasive paper or cabinet scraper

USEFUL ALTERNATIVES OR EXTRAS

Drill stand and electric drill for removing waste from mortises

Bench-top mortiser or portable router for cutting mortises

Miter saw with depth stop, band saw or radial arm saw for cutting tenon shoulders

1

MARKING OUT

1 The mortise is marked first and its length must be determined. This will not normally be less than half the width of the rail. It is important that the mortise does not go too close to the end of the frame since it will be in danger of breaking out. For this reason a

short extra length is often left on the piece, which is known as a horn, and is removed after assembly.

The mortise is often offset away from the outside, again to prevent it being too close to the end of the piece. In wider rails or T-shaped joints it will be in the center.

Mark the length of the mortise across the wood with the try square. Mortise-and-tenon joints are usually cut in sets and the joints marked out in groups to ensure that all the mortises are in the same place.

2 Mark the shoulders around the tenon with the try square. The length of the tenon is generally about two-thirds of the width of the rail. Start work on the face side or face edge and work round the piece, holding the square tight against the work for each side. If the last line meets up precisely with the first, the wood is accurately prepared and the tenon shoulders will be in line.

3 The width of the mortise is a little over one-third of the thickness of the rail. In practice, this is rounded up to the next chisel size.

Set the mortise gauge to the exact width of the chisel. This same setting will also be used to mark out the tenons, so the mortise gauge must be used carefully to avoid disturbing this adjustment.

Possible variations of the basic joint

There are different types of mortise-and-tenon joints, each appropriate in different situations. The through wedged-and-pegged version, for example, is entirely structural and appropriate for exterior joinery in particular.

In carcass work a number of mortise and tenons may be used in a line, connected by a narrow dado the same thickness as the tenon. The interpretations of the mortise and tenon are almost limitless and through being applied the joint to new situations it continues to evolve.

4 Once it is set to match the chisel width, use the mortise gauge to mark the position and thickness of both the mortise and the tenon.

On the piece that will have the tenon, start the mark on the edge of the rail, toward the end, along the end grain and along the opposite edge to the shoulder line. Hold the gauge against the face side of the work.

5 When marking the mortise, set the gauge to the middle of the rail. This is best done on an offcut of stock of the same dimensions as the work. Set the mortise gauge approximately using a metal rule. Working from both sides of the offcut, adjust the gauge until the marks it makes are the same from either side.

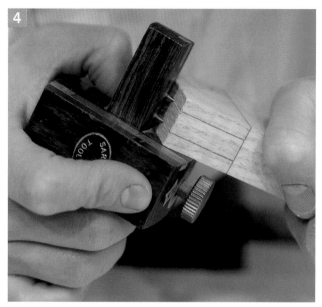

6 On the work itself, use the gauge from the face side only. The grooves made need to be clear and to stop at the pencil marks. If you are making a number of mortises, gauge them all at this stage.

Mark the width of the tenon with the marking gauge in a similar way to the cheeks, but work off the face edge rather than the face side.

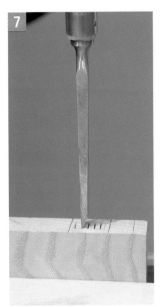

CUTTING THE MORTISE

7 The mortise is always cut first so that the tenon can be fitted to it later.

Secure the work firmly in a vise or use bench dogs or C-clamps to hold the job. Before beginning to cut the mortise, mark a line ⅛ inch (3 mm) in from the ends. This is an initial working line; once the mortise is to depth, trim the ends to give a neat finish.

The first work with the chisel is to make a row of shallow cuts at intervals of about 3/16 inch (5 mm). These must be at right angles to the sides of the mortise and act as a guide for the later stages of chopping out.

8 Work along the joint again with deeper cuts, and begin to lever out the chips as they become loose. The aim is to develop an action with the chisel that is firm but controlled – neither reluctant to cut nor likely to damage the work.

In the final stage it is helpful to stick a piece of masking tape around the chisel to mark the depth of the mortise. Continue chopping down until the required depth is reached, levering out the chips. The bottom of the joint can be scraped with the chisel.

9 Carefully pare back the ends of the joint with a freshly sharpened chisel. The lines marking the length of the mortise may be continued down the sides of the rail to provide a visual guide for the chisel and ensure that the ends of the mortise are vertical.

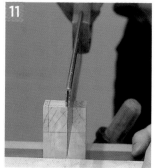

CUTTING THE TENON

10 Cut the tenon cheeks using a tenon saw. Set the work in the vise facing away from you at an angle of 45°. Cut down from the top corner along the end and face lines. Mark the area of waste to make sure that the saw cut is on the correct side of the line.

When the first two saw cuts have been made, turn the work around and repeat the process. As with all joints, efficient and accurate work is achieved through taking the time to get the job right first time rather than having to make adjustments later.

11 Set the work vertically in the vise to finish the saw cuts. The diagonal cuts already made will guide the saw, which is held horizontally. A few steady strokes will complete this part of the job. Finally, saw the sides of the tenon.

12 The shoulders are also cut with the tenon saw. Mount the work horizontally on the bench; bench dogs or C-clamps are best as they provide a positive

hold. A bench hook is adequate but does hold the piece of work less securely.

Start the saw cut at a slight downward angle and, once established, level it off. Repeat the process on the reverse side.

To cut the shoulders in the edges of the rail, clamp the work in the vise. Start the cut by rubbing the saw blade against the long shoulders that have already been cut.

ASSEMBLY

13 Clean up any waste or slight unevenness around the tenon shoulders using a chisel. Work from the edges into the middle of the joint to prevent tear-out at the corners.

14 The end of the tenon may be chamfered all round at this stage, if liked, to aid its entry into the mortise.

15 Check that the mortise-and-tenon joint fits on all four sides and that there is a small

tolerance for trapped glue at the bottom of the tenon. Rails have been known to split in cases where such an allowance has not been made.

Plane the inside edges of the rails to a finished surface as these will be inaccessible after assembly. This

Left *A mortise-and-tenon joint, ready for assembly*

removes any pencil marks. Apply glue to each surface with a brush and clamp up the joint with a sash clamp. Leave it to dry under pressure.

Finally, face off the complete joint using a smoothing plane at an angle of 45° to the grain to prevent damaging the surface; then finish the smoothing process using either abrasive paper or a cabinet scraper.

Miter joints

A MITER JOINT is formed when two pieces of wood are bevelled at the ends and joined to form a corner. The bevels are usually 45° and make a right-angled joint. As a simple glued joint the miter is not particularly strong, but it is appropriate for decorative applications such as mirror or picture frames.

Miters are common in carpentry in the fitting of molding and baseboards. When the work is attached to a wall the strength of the joint is not important. Miters are useful when making lippings for veneered work. In cabinetmaking

Each end is cut to 45° when making a square or rectangular frame

Miter joint *This joint is used where two pieces join at a 90° corner, each end being cut to an angle of 45°.*

the miter is often used for its visual effect as the joint exposes no visible end grain and allows the figure in the wood to continue round the frame without a visual break.

Making a miter joint

TOOLS & EQUIPMENT

Try square and pencil

Sliding bevel or 45° try square

Tenon saw

Masking/parcel tape

Piece of board, approximately ³/₄ x 4 x 10 inch (20 x 100 x 250 mm)

Smoothing plane

Clamping blocks and four C-clamps

Glue and brush

USEFUL ALTERNATIVES OR EXTRAS

Miter box for guiding a tenon saw through a rail at 45°

Frame miter saw with depth stop, fixed circular saw, or radial arm saw with tilting arbor for cutting miters

Sliding bevel or combination square is useful for marking angles other than 45°

MARKING OUT

1 Whether you intend using a miter box or saw, it is advisable to mark out the miter. This is essential if a jig is not used, but even if it is, laying out the work and marking the direction of the miter is important. If you are making a

frame, lay out the parts in pairs. Lay the top and bottom together and the sides likewise.

Mark the outside dimensions of the frame using a try square and pencil. It will be easier to cut the miter if you use stock that is slightly longer than its finished dimension.

2 Mark the miter using a sliding bevel set to 45° or a 45° try square. Again, mark the parts of the frame in pairs, holding them next to each other. Mark the 45° line from the outside extremity of the frame toward the center, forming a "V" at each end pointing toward each other. They are marked this way round to check that the inside of the miters correspond with one another.

3 Once both pairs of rails have been marked in this way, a jig can be used. For freehand cutting, however, additional marking is necessary. Using a 90° try square, mark lines across the edges of the rails from the ends of the miter.

Complete the marking with the 45° square on the reverse side of the rail. Working from the face edge of the stock, hold the square or bevel against the work and carefully mark a line from the outer tip of the miter.

SAWING

4 Sawing freehand, hold the work in the vise so that the miter is vertical. With a tenon saw positioned so that the blade is pointing up at about 45° and on the waste side of the marked line, begin the cut with a few short downward strokes. When the action is established, use longer forward strokes.

As the saw cut progresses, keep working to the waste side of the line and check that the reverse side of the joint is also being cut evenly. As the saw cut nears completion, revert to using short saw cuts to prevent tear-out on the inside edge of the miter. Wrapping a piece of masking or parcel tape around the base of the joint up to the edge mark is an effective added precaution.

Possible variations of the basic joint

The basic miter joint can be structurally improved by fitting dowels or biscuits (see pages 10–15). This not only strengthens the joint but also makes it easier to assemble.

A useful feature of the miter joint is that moldings, rabbets and grooves continue around the frame uninterrupted. This removes the need for complicated scribing.

TRUING UP

5 To true the miter, set the piece of work in the vise at 45° with the miter horizontal. Clamp a flat piece of board to the bench immediately behind the vise to act as a simple plane guide. Set the workpiece so that the marked line of the miter is exactly in line with the top of the board.

6 Resting the sole of the plane on the board, plane along the miter with the blade at a skew angle. This action reduces the risk of the plane damaging the tip of the miter while the guide board ensures a flat joint.

7 Set out the work on the bench to check that each joint fits. If adjustments have to be made,

remember that altering one joint will affect all the others. When removing stock from one joint, the one diagonally opposite will require evening up.

ASSEMBLY

8 The mitered frame may be glued together in one of two ways. The first method is to glue small triangular blocks to the

outside edge of each joint. These should be about half the size of the miter. The blocks form a flat surface across which a C-clamp can be applied.

The advantage of this system is that each joint is assembled separately under consistent pressure. Having set up the clamping blocks and C-clamps (one for each corner), work around the frame applying glue and clamping each joint in turn.

9 The second method of gluing the assembly together is more appropriate for light-duty applications such as picture frames. Four L-shaped blocks are required: for strength these should be made of plywood and have a groove running around the outside edge of each block that will accept string.

10 Lay out the frame and place a block at each corner. Pass strong string around the blocks and tie it off firmly. Twist a short stick into the string; the twisting action will pull the blocks together, bringing the joints under pressure.

In either case, a dry assembly run is advisable before you apply glue to the joints. If used, the glue blocks can be knocked or sawn off after assembly and the joint cleaned up with a smoothing plane.

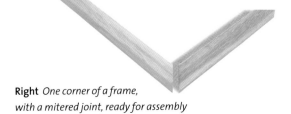

Right *One corner of a frame, with a mitered joint, ready for assembly*

Dado joints

DADO JOINTS are normally used in carcass work for fitting shelves and dividers. The dado (also called a housing) is a trench precisely cut to take another piece of wood, usually across the width of the work. The structural integrity of the dado joint is limited and it is dependent on a tight fit for its strength.

The basic joint runs right across the board but the dado can be stopped short of the face side of the job. The corresponding shelf or divider is notched to fit. This arrangement allows the interior work to be set back slightly from the carcass and generally produces a neater job.

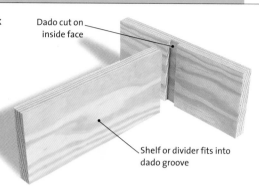

Dado cut on inside face

Shelf or divider fits into dado groove

Dado joint *A dado is a groove cut in the face of a component which will accommodate another member that fits in at right angles to it.*

Making a dado joint

TOOLS & EQUIPMENT

Try square and pencil

Marking gauge

Metal rule

Marking knife

C-clamps

Bevel-edged chisel

Tenon saw

Masking tape

Mallet

Manual router

Smoothing plane

Glue and brush

USEFUL ALTERNATIVES OR EXTRAS

Portable router or radial arm saw (with standard or dado head) for cutting dadoes

MARKING OUT

1 First establish the position of the dado and mark a line across the work using a try square and pencil. The width of the dado must be carefully measured. In a basic dado joint it will be marginally less than the board to be let in it.

Use a marking gauge to check the thickness of the shelf or divider and to see if the thickness is consistent across its width. The width of the dado will be slightly less than the setting of the marking gauge.

2 The depth of the dado should be about one-quarter to one-third of the thickness of the board; i.e., deep enough to make a strong joint but not deep enough to weaken the area around the dado. The depth

1

2

3

is set on the cutting gauge and scribed onto the edges of the dado joint.

3 Using a metal rule, measure the width of the dado from the first line and scribe both lines with a marking knife. Use a number of shallow strokes against the metal rule until the line is cut into the wood. A depth of 1/16 inch (2 mm) is about right.

Using the try square, mark lines from these incised lines on the face of the board down both edges. Draw them in pencil since they will be removed later.

SAWING

4 Secure the work to the bench with C-clamps before beginning the sawing. To provide a key for the saw, open up the scribed lines marking the width of the housing to a "V" with a chisel. Working by hand rather than with a mallet, and on the inside of the housing, hold the chisel at an angle of 45° to the face of the work. Hold the edge of the chisel parallel to the scribed line and 1/16 inch (2 mm) in from it. Push the chisel down into the incision.

Possible variations of the basic joint

A through or stopped dado joint can be modified by cutting a rabbet on one or both sides of the shelf or divider. This requires a narrower dado.

A dovetailed dado joint, as its name suggests, is a groove of dovetail section. The corresponding part of the joint has a dovetail tongue. This joint has great structural strength. To make a dovetailed dado joint by hand would be quite a challenge compared with using a portable router with a dovetail cutter.

Working along the line in steps the width of the chisel, open up the "V." When one side is complete, turn the work around to repeat the operation on the other side of the joint. The set of the tenon saw should just rest against the side of the incised line.

4

5

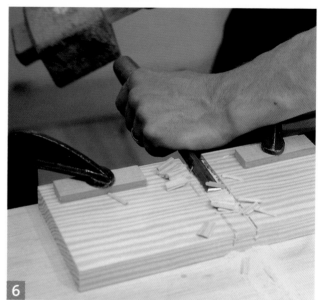

5 Begin the saw cut with the blade located in the "V" groove with the handle raised. When the sawing action is established, gradually bring the saw into a horizontal position without interrupting the cutting motion.

Continue the cut until the saw blade reaches the gauged lines at the bottom of the dado. It is helpful to mark the depth of the dado on the side of the saw blade with a strip of masking tape. During the sawing operation, check the lines on the side of the joint to ensure that the cut is vertical.

6

7

REMOVING WASTE

6 Remove the bulk of the waste using a chisel with a mallet. Work first from one edge with the chisel pointing up slightly and make a series of shallow cuts until the gauged depth mark is reached.

Turn the work around and repeat the operation. At this stage both ends of the housing should be at the correct depth with a shallow inverted "V" of material left in the middle of the housing.

In a short joint, i.e., one less than 8 inches (200 mm), this can be removed with a long chisel. Hold the chisel horizontally and pare down the waste in shallow

increments until the bottom of the housing is flat.

7 On a wider board a manual router is more accurate. This is a

simple tool consisting of a metal base with thumb plates cast into it. Through the base projects a blade, which is held in place with a screw that allows adjustment. The blade is L-shaped and ground to a sharp edge.

Set the blade to the depth of the dado. The base rests on the wood on either side of the dado and, as you push it along, the blade cleans up the joint to the preset depth.

Carry out the fitting of the joint and final trimming on the corresponding part. Plane the work carefully with a finely set smoothing plane to both finish the surface of the wood and trim the joint to fit snugly.

ASSEMBLY

8 The key to a good fit is constant checking until the joint is a firm push fit.

Using the marking gauge set to the depth of the dado, lightly mark a line around the end of the piece that enters the dado. This indicates the extent of the glue line. Stick masking tape up to the edge of each part of the joint.

Apply glue to both parts of the joint. A piece of softwood, slightly curved on one side, is a useful gluing aid. Place the curved side in contact with the work directly behind the dado. When the ends of the softwood piece are clamped up tight, it exerts pressure along the whole length of the joint.

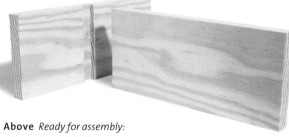

Above *Ready for assembly: a basic through dado joint, showing the joint running right across the board*

When the glue is dry, remove the clamps and tape and clean up the edges of the joint with a smoothing plane.

Dovetail joints

THE DOVETAIL is an ancient joint going back to Egyptian times. It has a configuration that makes it impossible to pull apart in one direction and, because of the large surface area of contact between the pieces, is very strong all round.

The applications of the dovetail are diverse and it is used by musical instrument-makers and boat builders, as well as joiners and cabinetmakers. In furniture, its most visible application is in drawer making. It is also widely used in traditional cabinet construction. The fundamental advantage of the dovetail is its strength, but the nature of the joint also gives it a strong visual appeal.

A number of jigs are available for making dovetails. These are usually designed for use with a portable router, the better jigs being rather expensive. Good as these may be, cabinetmakers do take great pride in the quality of their hand-cut dovetails and

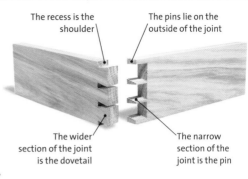

The recess is the shoulder

The pins lie on the outside of the joint

The wider section of the joint is the dovetail

The narrow section of the joint is the pin

The dovetail joint *This joint comprises two parts: the dovetails, named for their fan shape, and the pins, which fit in between and form the top and bottom of the joint. The dovetails are usually bigger than the pins. The ratio of the bevel on the dovetails is generally 6:1 in softwoods and 8:1 in hardwoods.*

regard them as an indication of level of skill. Machine-cut dovetails are certainly strong and efficient but just do not feel the same.

Constructing a through dovetail joint

TOOLS & EQUIPMENT

Marking or cutting gauge

Sliding bevel

Pencil

Small try square

Dovetail saw

Coping saw

C-clamps

Plywood panel, approximately 6 x 12 inch to protect the bench

Short cutoffs, 1 inch (25 mm) square and slightly longer than the width of the joint

Bevel-edged chisel

Mallet

Small marking knife

Hammer

Masking tape

Glue and brush

Smoothing plane

USEFUL ALTERNATIVES OR EXTRAS

Dovetail templates instead of sliding bevel

Gent's orjeweler's saw for removing waste on fine dovetails

Dovetail jigs plus portable router with bushing and dovetail bit

MARKING OUT THE DOVETAILS

1 Set the gauge to slightly more than the thickness of the stock and scribe a line around each end of the joint. The cutting gauge is preferable here to the marking gauge because it has a small knife rather than a point, which produces a clean-cut line on cross-grain work.

2 The spacing of the joints is largely a question of structural and aesthetic balance. The outer pins should not be too small or they could break off. Account must be made of the spacings of the pins as well as the dovetails.

Possible variations of the basic joint

As with the mortise-and-tenon joint, the dovetail joint has almost endless possible permutations. The through dovetail described here is the simplest of them, but none the less it offers considerable scope for variation. Altering the number, size and spacing of the dovetails in a given width will change the whole appearance of the job. Similarly, experimenting with contrasting woods for dovetails and pins and with different sizes of dovetail in the same joint is likely to generate some exciting effects visually.

Use a sliding bevel to mark the dovetails. Set it to the appropriate angle and hold it against the end of the work, penciling in the lines required. Shade the waste spaces in between the dovetails to indicate the parts to be removed and to ensure that the saw cuts are made on the correct side of the line. (Use a small metal try square to mark the line across the end of the joint.)

CUTTING THE DOVETAILS

3 Clamp the work at a height comfortable for sawing. To keep the work firm in the vise, hold a piece of scrap wood behind it as support. A good posture is essential for accurate sawing, and ideally the top of the work-piece should be at elbow height. Begin sawing the dovetails with the saw pointing upward for two or three strokes. Once the sawing rhythm is established, level out the saw, maintaining a steady action and cutting down to the scribed line. It is easier to cut all the right-hand sides first, followed by the left-hand sides.

4 Remove the bulk of the waste using a coping saw (or using a jeweler's saw for fine work). Start the cut in line with the dovetail bevel and, after a few strokes, work round to the horizontal. The aim is to remove as much waste as possible, not touching the scribed line.

5 To remove the outside waste, clamp the work horizontally in the vise and saw to the scribed line with the dovetail saw.

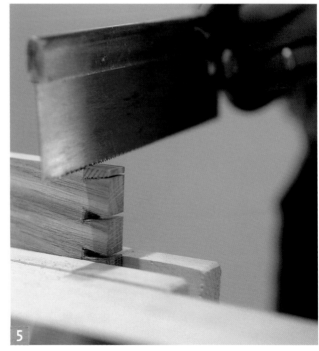

6 To trim the joint, clamp the work to the bench with a piece of plywood beneath the job in order both to protect the bench and to prevent tear-out on the reverse side of the joint. Clamp a square section cutoff on top of the workpiece, in line with the scribed line at the base of the dovetail joint.

7 Holding the chisel firmly against the guide block, tap the handle with a mallet.

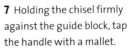

MARKING OUT THE PINS

8 To mark out the pins, hold the work vertically in the vise and about 1 inch (25 mm) proud of the vise top. Place a piece of scrap behind the work so that the dovetails can rest level. Hold the dovetails firmly in position and scribe off the pins using a small knife. Fill the scribed lines in with a sharp pencil straight away as they can be difficult to see.

Continue the pencil lines around to the face of the work, holding the try square against the end of the work; again shade the waste areas. Both sides of the work may be marked out in this way, although it is not strictly necessary.

CUTTING THE PINS

9 Saw the pins in the same manner as the dovetails. Great accuracy is called for as there is no margin for error. Care and a steady hand will produce a good result. It is easier to cut the pins to the line to start with rather than leaving waste to be trimmed back later.

The removal of the waste again calls for the coping saw. Keep checking the position of the coping saw blade at the back of the joint to make sure that it is not wandering too close to the scribed line. Allowance has to be made at the beginning and end of each cut for the beveled shape of the pins.

Set up the work to trim back the waste to the base of the joint as before. The wider area to be cleaned up requires more care than the small spaces between the dovetails. Cutting back to the guide block in one operation may damage the end grain, affecting both the efficiency and the neatness of the joint. To prevent this, pare the joint back gradually, pushing down on the chisel by hand, leaving about 1/16 inch (2 mm) proud of the guide block. Make the final cut by holding the chisel against the block and tapping the handle of the chisel with the mallet.

ASSEMBLY

10 Clamp the pin section of the joint vertically in the vise. Ensure that the dovetail part of the joint

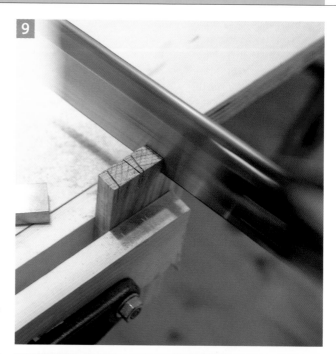

is in the correct relative position and check for fit. Do this by tapping with a hammer on to a block of wood resting on the dovetails. This applies firm even pressure across the joint without causing damage. If the joint starts to go together evenly, it will require no further attention. Do not fully assemble the joint at this stage.

If the joint does not fit evenly, note the tight spots and gradually ease them back with a chisel, checking often for fit. Dovetails should be tight but clearly not so tight that they split.

Apply masking tape to the joint up to the glue lines. Brush glue evenly over all parts of the joint that will be in contact with others, ensuring that the surfaces of the joint are "wetted," i.e., the glue soaks in. This helps to create a good bond.

11 Finally, assemble the joint using the block and hammer to drive it home. Most modern glues work best when allowed to dry under pressure and clamping is advisable.

12 Once the glue is dry, remove the tape. Clamp the work firmly for cleaning up. Using a finely tuned smoothing plane, work at an angle of 45° from the outside to the inside of the joint. This cutting angle overcomes the problem of differing grain directions and the job should require only a light sanding.

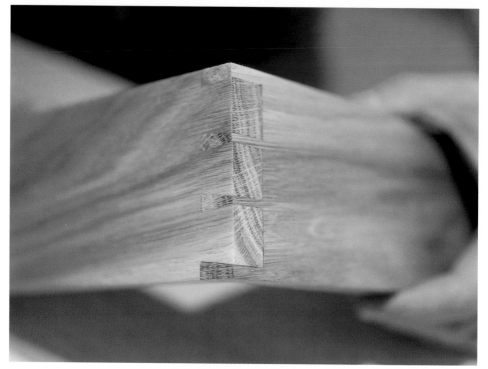

13 Hand-cut dovetails are a true delight. The accurate marking of the pins is one of the secrets of a neat dovetail joint. This is accomplished by scribing the pins directly off the corresponding dovetail part of the joint. Alternatively, the pins may be cut first and used to scribe off the tails. Only through practice will you find your own preferred method of working.

Above *Neatly corresponding dovetails and pins, ready to be glued and hammered home in a tight-fitting right-angled joint*

Projects

ONCE YOU HAVE MASTERED jointmaking, you are ready to move on to the exciting part – actually making something from wood. The projects here comprise an attractive occasional table topped with glass, which employs cross-lap joints; a mirror frame that relies on miter joints and has an unusual veneer corner detail and a wooden tray that features attractive dovetail joints. When you are feeling more adventurous, you can move on to tackle the lap joints of the bookcase. This project requires more equipment and a little more time than the other three, but can still be accomplished by a beginner in four to five days.

Glass-topped table

THIS DECORATIVE TABLE is a straightforward project, which uses cross-lap joints and can be made in a weekend by a beginner. Because the components are so small – 1 inch square – a relatively hard wood is needed. The table here is of North American maple, which is remarkably stable and very strong, but it could just as easily have been made in oak, cherry or ash. Softwood and lighter, more springy wood such as walnut are less suitable, as the components would be more inclined to flex and give a slightly unstable structure.

The ends of the rails and the tops of the legs may be left square or planed into pyramid shapes as illustrated here. Once the glass is put

in place in the wooden structure, triangular shapes are created throughout the design, and this pyramid-shaped detailing enhances the design theme.

The glass tops are ¼ inch (6 mm) thick, have ground and polished beveled edges and fit squarely on the table frame. If preferred, larger pieces of glass can be used, positioned diagonally. The glass rests either directly on the finished wood or upon domed-shaped rubber bump stops, available from hardware stores.

Plans

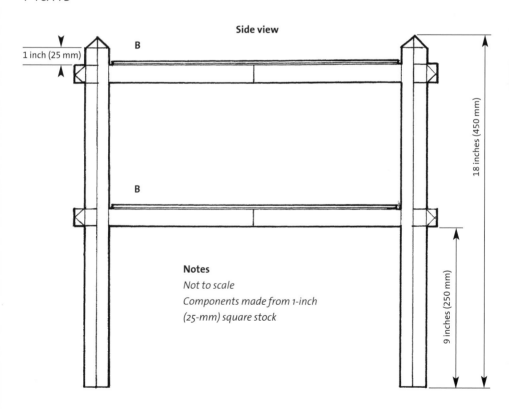

Side view

1 inch (25 mm)

B

B

18 inches (450 mm)

9 inches (250 mm)

Notes
Not to scale
Components made from 1-inch (25-mm) square stock

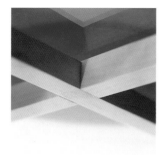

CUTTING LIST AND MATERIALS

Component	Quantity	Finished dimensions
A Legs	4	1 x 1 x 18 inches (25 x 25 x 460 mm)
B Rails	4	1 x 1 x 28¾ inches (25 x 25 x 730 mm)
Glass tops*	2	¼ inch (6 mm) thick
Suggested lumber		North American maple
Suggested finish		Wax, shellac or Danish oil
Alternative lumber		A hardwood such as oak, cherry or ash

Notes

*10 dome-shaped rubber bump stops on which to rest the glass are optional.

*It is advisable not to order the glass until the table framework has been assembled.

Above *Detail of the lap joint used to join the cross rails*

Opposite *The pyramid-shaped detail on the ends of the rails provides an interesting effect*

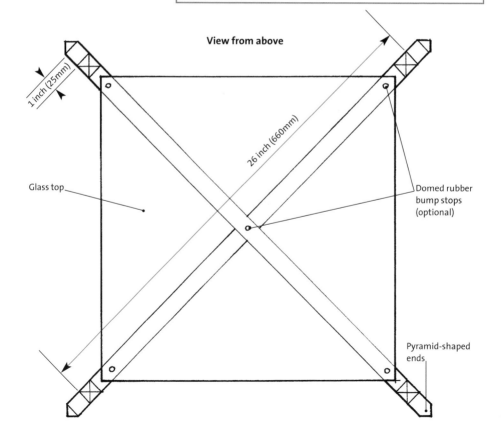

View from above

1 inch (25mm)

26 inch (660mm)

Glass top

Domed rubber bump stops (optional)

Pyramid-shaped ends

Above *Glass-topped table, made from North American maple, using cross-lap joints*

Right *Detail showing the subtle intersections between glass and wooden frame*

Far right *Detail showing the glass supported on the rails, by rubber bump stops*

Construction

TOOL LIST

Smoothing plane

Marking knife

Pencil and try square

Marking gauge

Backsaw (large dovetail or small tenon saw)

C-clamps and clamping blocks

Chisel

Mallet

Plunge router

Block plane

Abrasive paper and cork sanding block

Glue and brush

Fast-acting clamps

PREPARING THE WOOD

1 Having machined all the components for the table to dimension, remove all of the machine marks made by the planer by trimming all the surfaces with a smoothing plane. This is done at this stage because cross-lap joints need to be snug and tight, and cleaning up at a later stage risks opening up an otherwise tight joint.

MARKING AND CUTTING THE JOINTS

2 Assemble the components on the workbench and mark up the shoulders using a marking knife or pencil and a try square (see pages 6–7). Because there are two sets of four identical components, it is efficient and more accurate to mark up each set of four at the same time.

3 Having marked the positions of the shoulders, gauge the depth of each cross-lap joint using a marking gauge. Your objective is to mark up, and then cut to your line, a joint that is slightly tight across its width so that with one or two shaves of the plane that tightness can be relieved.

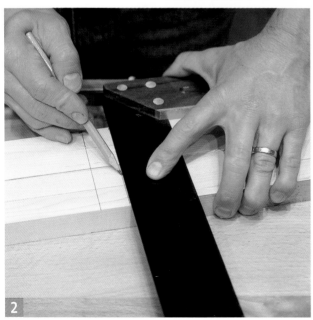

4 You need to make sure that the backsaw (a large dovetail or a small tenon saw) cuts with the kerf in the waste side of the cut.

Take the sensible precaution of first deepening the gauge line across your component by enlarging it with a marking knife and then taking a small V-shaped paring with a chisel on the waste side of your gauge line. This gives an exaggerated "V" with one vertical shoulder and provides an accurate start to the sawing by enabling your saw to sit inside the "V," snug up against the vertical shoulder.

REMOVING THE WASTE

5 Once you have sawn down each of the shoulders in turn, use a chisel with a mallet to remove the waste material in between them down to the gauge line. Work from either side of the cross-lap, paring slightly upward to eliminate the danger of going below the gauge line on the far side. You can if you wish do one or two saw cuts in the middle of the

waste of the cross-lap to give you a "depth stop," or a sense of how near you are to the gauge line on either side.

6 When you have finished paring the bottom of all of the necessary components, you are ready to begin to fit them.

ALTERNATIVE METHODS

7 Although the sawing and chiseling of cross-lap joints of this type can be a good exercise, you may wish to cut some of these components at one go using a plunge router. This will greatly reduce the time taken to make the project. Assemble a set of four identical components and clamp a board across them to create a guide for the router. In this way one shoulder is routed and the base of the cross-lapped joint can be cut on four of the components with one machine setting. You may need to make two or three passes of the router in order to achieve the full depth of the joint.

To cut the opposite shoulder you could set up a second fence, or a less accurate option would be to move the first fence to a second position.

ENSURING A GOOD FIT

8 Now go for a trial fit. Because you have sawn or cut the shoulders slightly tight, your first attempt at fitting one component into the other may well be unsuccessful. Do not force the fit; instead, using a bench plane, take a stopped shaving off one or both sides of the necessary component.

9 By planing each side you will gradually open up the joint so do this carefully, one shave at a time, until you have a perfect fit.

SHAPING THE ENDS

10 Next mark out the pyramid-shaped ends on all components except the feet. Pencil a line ³/₈ inch (10 mm) from the end or at your chosen depth, all the way around the base of each pyramid. Then mark a diagonal cross on the end of each component.

11 Remove the waste with a small backsaw; then plane the end grain down to the fine pencil lines using a smoothing plane or a small block plane.

PREFINISHING

12 Since all the components will have been lightly planed before jointing, they should need only light sanding prior to finishing. Start by using a 120 or 150 grit backed by a cork sanding block; then move through the finer grits to 180 grit. Maple is a very dense hardwood and will take an exceptionally fine finish, so if you have the time and patience,

sand right through to 320 grit. For wood that has been smoothed with a hand plane, however, 180 grit – or possibly 150 – is all that is needed when cleaning up. Certainly for adhesion purposes do not use finer than 240 grit if you intend to finish with coats of lacquer.

13 The light, contemporary look of maple can be retained by using a transparent rather than a yellowing finish. Wax is the easiest finish to apply and scarcely changes the color of the wood. Although it gives the wood very little protection from finger marks or hot liquids, wax could be used to finish this particular project since the glass surface will protect the wood to an extent. An alternative is to give the table frame a light sealing coat of transparent shellac or two or three coats of thin Danish oil.

Apply your chosen finish to all the components with a soft cloth, taking care to first mask off all the areas of your joints that will be receiving glue.

ASSEMBLY STAGES

14 Plan the assembly of your table as follows: the first stage will involve the two cross frames, each of which has two rails to take the glass shelves. There is a lap joint in the middle of each cross frame, plus another four, one on each end to accept the legs. Remember that these are in a different plane to the one that you cut at the center. Construct the four legs, which will have two lap joints on each, one to take the top cross frame and shelf and one for the lower cross frame.

Try a dry assembly and if all the joints look good, plan to assemble first the cross frames and then, when these are dry, the legs. The wooden structure of the table will then be complete. For each joint apply a

little glue to each component, covering all the meeting faces. Then bring each joint together.

15 Apply a fast-acting clamp to each joint as you form it, squeezing the clamp down until glue just comes out of the joint. Do not wipe it away but let it dry.

16 Because the exterior surfaces have been waxed or oiled, the glue will not stick very well and can be gently eased away when dry with a small paring chisel.

17 Finally, fit the self-adhesive rubber bump stops – five on each shelf – if using.

18 Place the glass on top to complete your table.

Mirror frame

MITER JOINTS are most often seen in decorative frames where the visual effect is important. The miter is structurally quite adequate for this type of work, although some form of reinforcement is usually incorporated. This project features keys in the joints to strengthen them.

The contrasting strip of decorative veneer, although technically a laminate, gives the impression of an inlay.

Little wood is required for this project, and any hardwood may be used. Small projects of this kind provide an ideal opportunity to use rare or exotic wood, difficult to justify in larger jobs. The frame shown here is in American cherry with black walnut veneer. It would serve just as well as a picture frame or could be scaled up for a much bigger mirror.

Above *Detail of the corner of the frame, showing a well-fitted miter, the veneer keys used to reinforce the joint and the decorative veneer line*

TOOLS & EQUIPMENT

Glue and brush

Four C-clamps

Smoothing plane

Pencil and try square

Sliding bevel

Tenon or miter saw

Chisel

Picture-frame clamp

Marking gauge

Fine abrasive paper

Cabinet scraper

Pin hammer

Molding pins and nail punch

CUTTING LIST AND MATERIALS

Component	Quantity	Finished dimensions
A Frame sides	2	¾ x 1 x 13 inches (20 x 25 x 330 mm)
B Side rabbets	2	⅜ x ⅜ x 13 inches (10 x 10 x 330 mm)
C Frame ends	2	¾ x 1 x 9 inches (20 x 25 x 230 mm)
D End rabbets	2	⅜ x ⅜ x 9 inches (10 x 10 x 230 mm)
E Frame laminates and corner keys		
	5	³⁄₆₄ x ⅞ x 14 inches (1 x 22 x 355 mm)
F Clamping blocks		
	2	¾ x ¾ x 14 inches (20 x 20 x 355 mm)
	1	⅜ x ⅜ x 14 inches (10 x 10 x 355 mm)
G Backing panel	1	¹⁄₁₆ x 9 x 13 inches (2 x 230 x 330 mm)
Suggested lumber		A, B, C and D – American cherry
		E – Black walnut veneer
		F – Scrap stock
		G – Medium-density fiberboard
Suggested finish		Danish oil, polyurethane varnish or wax
Alternative lumber		Hardwood such as rosewood and sycamore veneer, or ash and brown oak veneer
Notes		
It is advisable not to order the glass until the frame has been assembled. Eyes and hanging wire are required to complete the project		

Plans

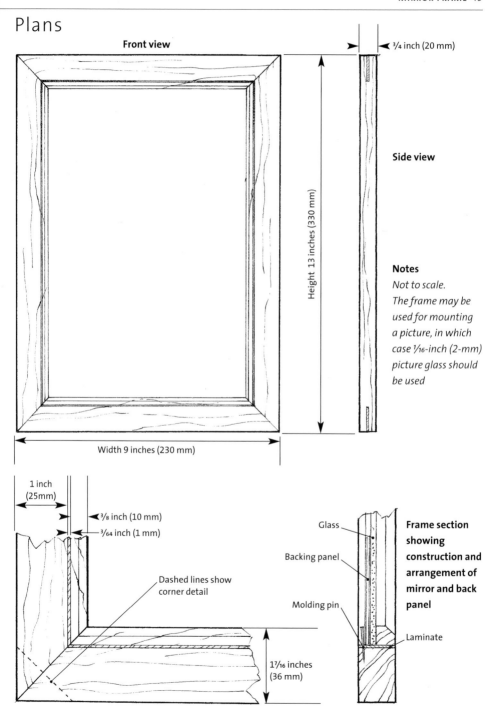

Front view

Height 13 inches (330 mm)

Width 9 inches (230 mm)

¾ inch (20 mm)

Side view

Notes
*Not to scale.
The frame may be
used for mounting
a picture, in which
case ¹⁄₁₆-inch (2-mm)
picture glass should
be used*

1 inch (25mm)

³⁄₈ inch (10 mm)

³⁄₆₄ inch (1 mm)

Dashed lines show
corner detail

1⁷⁄₁₆ inches
(36 mm)

Glass

Backing panel

Molding pin

**Frame section
showing
construction and
arrangement of
mirror and back
panel**

Laminate

Above *View from behind, showing the pin that fixes in the MDF back, and the fitting of the eyes and hanging wire*

Top *Detail showing the effect of light on the chamfer and the contrast of the veneer line*

Left *Mitered mirror frame made from American cherry and black walnut veneer*

Construction

PREPARING THE SECTIONS

1 The frame section is formed by gluing together the veneer, rabbets and rails. (The rails are the frame components and the rabbets are the narrow strips of wood that create a rabbet joint.)

Apply glue to both the strip of veneer and the rails. Lay the clamping blocks on either side of the assembly and apply the clamps. Repeat the process for the other three strips. Carefully trim the edges of the veneer flush with the rail using the smoothing plane.

2 The process for gluing the rabbets is the same, but there is little margin for error. The top of the assembled section must be flush and carefully clamped. Wipe the excess glue off while it is still wet.

3 Plane all round the four assembled sections to clean up

glue marks and any unevenness, being careful to remove a minimum of stock.

Mark the chamfers in pencil, and then chamfer the inside edge of the frame with the smoothing plane at a consistent 45° angle. Set the plane to a fine cut and remove the same number of shavings from each piece.

MAKING THE JOINTS

4 Mark out the miters following the techniques described on pages 22–23. Accuracy is particularly important if the laminated strips are to line up properly in the finished job. Ensure that the rabbets are on the inside of the work.

5

6

action of the plane does not distort the frame and risk fracturing one of the joints.

Finish the edges similarly – this time with the frame held in the vise. Work from the corners toward the center to avoid damaging the fine corners of the joints. Remove glue on the inside corners with a chisel.

FITTING THE CORNER KEYS

7 The keys are fitted into slots cut with the tenon saw. Mark the positions for these by drawing lines across the outside edges of the frame 1 inch (25 mm) from the corner. Set the marking gauge to half the thickness of the frame and scribe a line around the corner between the two pencil lines.

5 Cut the miters using one of the methods described previously (see pages 22–23). The miter saw shown here has a fine-tooth blade which, when the work is held firmly in place, gives a clean and accurate cut and avoids the potential tear-out from a tenon saw. Although the joint may be glued from a miter saw cut, trimming the miter with a smoothing plane gives a neater result and makes the most of the fine details where the veneers meet.

Remove any excess glue from inside the rabbet with a chisel.

ASSEMBLY

6 Clamp the frame dry first to check the fits of the miters and to rehearse the clamping procedure for the gluing stage. A fast-acting clamp (illustrated) speeds up and simplifies the clamping process but is not essential. C-clamps are also useful here, where perfect alignment is required. Assembling the joints individually makes the procedure easier.

Apply glue to the joints (see pages 24– 25). When the glue is thoroughly dry, clean the faces of the frame with the smoothing plane, first clamping the work securely to the bench so that the

8 Clamp the work in the vise with one miter pointing upward. The saw cut must be straight and the bottom of the slot cut flat. Remove all the dust from the slot.

7

Cut a piece of veneer about 2 inches (50 mm) long and check for fit. It should fit fairly easily without being forced. If it is too tight, sand by rubbing it on a piece of abrasive paper laid flat on the bench. Keep checking until a good fit is obtained. Glue both sides of the key and push it into place, making sure that it rests on the bottom of the slot.

9 Trim the veneer back with the tenon saw; then plane it flush with the frame. Repeat for the other three miters.

FINISHING

10 The finish on fine work is very important and the first stage is surface preparation. On finely grained wood it is best to use a cabinet scraper, but fine abrasive paper and a sanding block may be used. Take care not to round over the corners, other than to take off their sharpness.

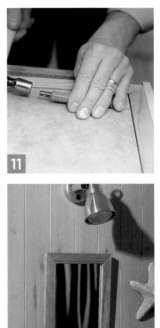

The chosen finish should enhance the natural contrast of the color in the wood. The Danish oil used here quickly builds up a low to medium luster.

11 Use a piece of thin MDF as a backing panel for the mirror, securing it with molding pins. These are easier to fit if a nail punch is used. Leave about ¼ inch (6 mm) protruding.

Fit eyes on either side of the frame to take a hanging wire. Position the eyes approximately one-third of the way down each side of the frame.

Bookcase

THIS BOOKCASE IS relatively straightforward to make and can be accomplished by a beginner in four to five days. An attractive and useful piece of furniture, it is made here in English ash. Many different woods could be used, however – hardwood or softwood – although cutting clean shoulders on the shelves and housings is more difficult in softwood. You could also consider making the bookcase with light-colored carcass sides and stained dark shelves.

The design of the bookcase features large, curved, heavy 3½-inch (90-mm)- thick side components. These are made by laminating together two 1¾-inch (45-mm)- thick pieces, obtained from sawn stock, 2 inches (50 mm) thick.

Begin making the project by preparing these thick vertical sides. Plane a face side on each and glue these face sides together. Apply glue to both surfaces and apply pressure evenly all round. Unless you have a press, you will need to use about 20 C- or fast-acting clamps and position them around each laminated component, roughly 4 inches (100 mm) apart. When the glue has cured, work a new face side and face edge. Then set a marking gauge to the required thickness of the component (3½ inches), mark all round and plane to thickness. Mark the width of the uprights (9¾ inches) and plane. Then use a square and rule to mark the length (37½ inches), saw and plane the end grain. You are now ready for Step 1 (see page 57).

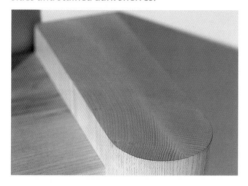

Above *The TG boards are fixed with screws from the rear and sit in a rabbet*

Top *Detail of the bold curve on the front of the thick sides of the bookcase*

CUTTING LIST AND MATERIALS

Component	Quantity	Finished dimensions
A Sides	2	3½ x 9¾ x 37½ inch (90 x 245 x 950 mm)
B Shelves	4	⅞ x 8 x 28½ inch (22 x 200 x 720 mm)
C Plinth	1	⅞ x 3 x 28½ inch (22 x 75 x 720 mm)
D Back – TG	8	⅜ x 3¾ x 32½ inch (10 x 95 x 825 mm)
Suggested lumber		A, B and C – Ash; D*
Suggested finish		Danish oil
Alternative lumber		A hardwood such as cherry or maple, or a softwood such as parana pine

Notes

*Choose a hardwood with a strong figure such as oak or chestnut, or use a softwood such as parana pine. If you do not have the equipment to make your own tongue-and-groove panels purchase ready-made boards from your lumber supplier.

Plans

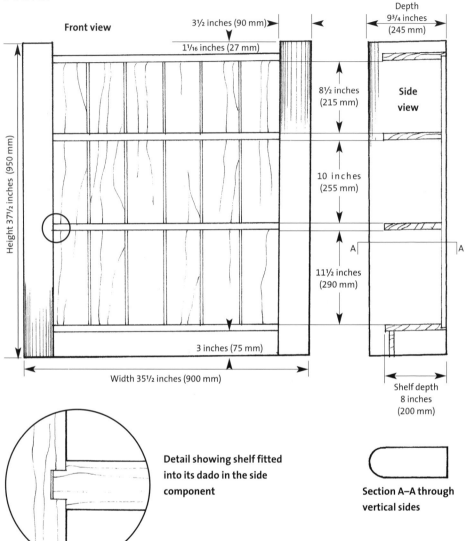

Front view

3½ inches (90 mm)

1¹/₁₆ inches (27 mm)

Height 37½ inches (950 mm)

8½ inches (215 mm)

Side view

Depth
9¾ inches (245 mm)

10 inches (255 mm)

11½ inches (290 mm)

3 inches (75 mm)

Width 35½ inches (900 mm)

Shelf depth
8 inches (200 mm)

A—A

Detail showing shelf fitted into its dado in the side component

Section A–A through vertical sides

Notes

Not to scale

Laminated side components made from two 1¾-inch (45-mm) pieces

Shelves ⅞ inch (22 mm) thick

3¾-inch (95-mm) tongue-and-groove boards for back rabbeted into edge

Right *Detail at the base of the bookcase, showing the bottom shelf and plinth*

Far right *Tongue-and-groove board with molding detail on the edges are used for the back of the bookcase*

Below *Stout bookcase with curved sides made from ash*

Construction

TOOLS & EQUIPMENT

Glue and brush

Twenty C- or fast-acting clamps

Marking gauge

Try square

Steel rule

Bench saw

Pencil

Table saw or band saw

Jack or smoothing plane

Gooseneck scraper

Abrasive paper and curved sanding block

Panel gauge

Marking knife

Chisel

Tenon saw

Masking tape

Plunge router

Paring chisel

Shoulder plane

8 sash clamps, at least 40 inches (1000 mm) long, and clamping blocks

Electric sander or smoothing plane

Cork sanding block

Molding plane

Screws and screwdriver

MOLDING THE FRONT OF THE SIDES

1 Having prepared the side components (see page 54), shape the molding on the front of them. First mark out the shape in pencil on the end grain. Then remove the waste, either

by passing it across the table saw with the saw blade tilted over to 45°, or by using a band saw with the table tilted to 45°.

Once most of the waste has been removed in this way, approach the marked line by planing a series of parallel flats that gradually approach the line as more and more facets are planed on to the end.

Finally, smooth around the molding on each component using a curved scraper known as a gooseneck. Then finish off using abrasive paper backed by a curved sanding block.

CUTTING OUT THE HOUSINGS

2 Carefully mark the position of the dadoes, or housings, that will accept the shelves on the sides of the uprights. Mark out both uprights at the same time, using the rear of each as your reference surface.

3 Use a square to mark lines at right angles to your reference surface, and a large marking gauge, called a panel gauge, to mark the stopped front of the dadoes for the shelves.

4 Clamp a steel rule on the position of each dado shoulder and then scribe across using a marking knife, with the beveled side facing the waste side of your cut. Make deep cuts so that the saw cuts the shoulders in the right place. Remove the rule and pare a "V" groove to the waste side of the lines, using a chisel. This allows the saw to sit snugly against each vertical shoulder.

5 Mark a small tenon saw with masking tape to indicate the depth of your dadoes; then saw down to this depth to form the dadoes on both uprights.

6 Alternatively, an easier and more accurate way to cut a dado is to use a plunge router, which cuts both the shoulders and the base of the dado in one operation. Guided by scrap clamped across the job, a router can cut each dado fairly quickly with two or three passes, increasing the depth with each cut.

Securely clamp your job to the bench; then, working from back to front, pare the waste material of each dado using a paring chisel angled slightly upward.

The front, or stopped, end of the dado is the most difficult to finish off. Here you have to chisel vertical shoulders and pare into them as best you can.

Originally, the manual router was used to work the bottom of dadoes like this, but this has now been largely replaced by the electric router.

FITTING THE SHELVES

7 Cut the shoulders on the ends of the plinth and the shelves ³⁄₈ inch (10 mm) from the end of each component. These, too, are most successfully cut with a router, using either a rabbet cutter or a straight cutter guided by scrap clamped across the job, or by guiding the router off the end grain of each shelf.

Since a dado joint's strength depends on a very snug fit, route the shoulders slightly tight and then plane with a shoulder plane to fit snugly.

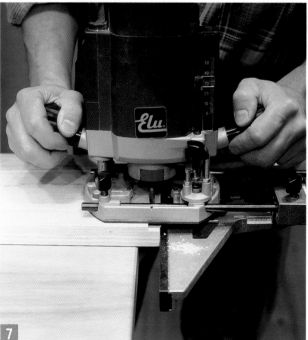

9 Now that you know that each individual joint fits, you need to check that they all fit at the same time in the same way. If they do not, take a step back and examine whether the lengths of your shelves are all exactly the same and the positions of your dadoes are all in good relation to one another.

At the same time, do a dry assembly to work out how you are going to assemble the carcass and where you are going to require clamping pressure. A carcass of this size will require eight sash clamps of at least 40 inches (1000 mm) in length.

8 Test the fit of the plinth ends and shelf ends in their dadoes. They should not be so tight that they require hammering home, nor should they rattle around in their dadoes.

You will now need to cut the rabbets into which the back panels will fit. A simple rabbet is needed on the rear edge of the top and bottom shelves, while there is a stopped rabbet on the inside rear edges of the sides. You also need to cut the mortises that will accept the ends of the plinth.

PREFINISHING

10 First, mask with tape all the areas that will be receiving glue. Apply the tape and trim it carefully with a knife – this is essential since it protects the gluing areas from the finishing oil that would prevent the glue from adhering well.

11 Next, remove all of the existing machine marks and any surface defects. If your components have come straight from the planer, you need to remove the slight ripple marks left by the planer. Do this either by using a sanding machine or by first passing over the job with a smoothing plane to plane out all of the machine marks and then going over all of the surfaces with abrasive paper.

If you are sanding by hand, start with 120-grit abrasive backed by a cork sanding block and sand carefully in line with the grain of the lumber. When you are convinced that the finish is as good as you can get with 120-grit abrasive, move on to 150-grit and then to 180-grit. You will spend less and less time with each grade of abrasive paper, but it is important that you remove all of the marks and

scratches of the preceding grade before moving on to the next one.

12 Apply two or three thin coats of Danish oil with a soft cloth, but bear in mind that the sheen is due not to the oil but to previous careful preparation of the surface. All you are doing with the Danish oil is enhancing the original scratch-free surface that you prepared with the abrasive paper.

ASSEMBLY

13 Once the components have been finished and polished, carry out a dry assembly with the top and bottom shelves in place, using clamps and clamping blocks to protect the finished surface of the wood. Check that the carcass is square by measuring the diagonals, and adjust if necessary.

Carefully paint glue on the surfaces and then bring them together. If using PVA glue, make sure that you apply this in a cool room and work relatively quickly. You have about five minutes of "open" time before the glue starts to gel and becomes less workable. If you want a longer "open" time, use a resin glue.

Once the carcass has been

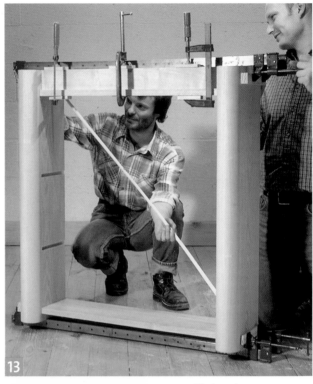

assembled, apply pressure evenly, again being careful to protect the prefinished surfaces. Just squeeze so that each joint snugs up. Check again that the carcass is square. When it is all glued, do not try to wipe off any glue that has squeezed out; just walk away and leave the glue to harden.

14 When the glue has partly cured, use a chisel to remove the excess. It should come away easily since it will not have stuck very well to the prefinished, oiled surface.

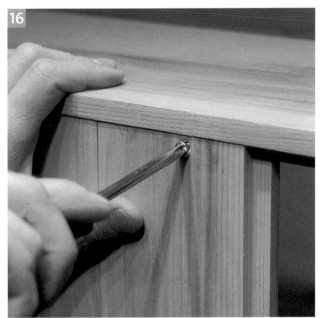

15 Now prepare the materials for the back, which when fitted will hold the bookcase square. The tongues can be made as shown with a molding plane. A router with a suitable cutter could also be used, or if you wish, buy ready-made tongue and grooving. Sand and finish these back panels.

16 Fix the tongue-and-groove panels in the rabbets on the back of the top and bottom shelves and on the uprights, using a screw in the middle of each board. You will have to reduce the width of the end boards for a symmetrical pattern.

Use Danish oil to finish inside the tongues and grooves of the panels. This is because each panel will expand and contract slightly around the fixing point, exposing wood inside the tongue-and-groove joint.

Finally, clean down and check the oil finish, reoiling as needed.

Breakfast tray

THIS PROJECT makes full use of the single dovetail joint, the dovetail construction here serving as both the structure and the decoration of the piece. The construction is of four strips of wood for the ends and sides, two blocks for the handles and one piece of veneered plywood for the base.

The size of the tray can be varied to suit individual requirements. The type of wood used is a matter of personal preference, but a hardwood is more satisfactory than a softwood for cutting the joints. A contrasting wood for the handles accentuates the dovetail feature. The base should match either the frame or the handles.

Since the parts are small, the cutoff bin of a lumber supplier may well provide you with some interesting and low-cost stock.

Above *One of the tray's handles – the dovetail detail emphasizes the joint at each corner of the tray*

Plans

Plan – view from above

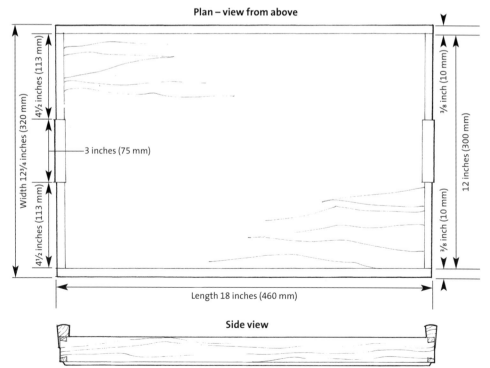

4½ inches (113 mm)

3 inches (75 mm)

4½ inches (113 mm)

Width 12¾ inches (320 mm)

⅜ inch (10 mm)

⅜ inch (10 mm)

12 inches (300 mm)

Length 18 inches (460 mm)

Side view

CUTTING LIST AND MATERIALS

Component	Quantity	Finished dimensions
A Sides	2	³⁄₈ x 1¼ x 18 inches (10 x 30 x 460 mm)
B Ends	2	³⁄₈ x 1¼ x 12 inches (10 x 30 x 300 mm)
C Handles*	1	⁵⁄₈ x 1¼ x 12 inches (15 x 30 x 300 mm)
D Base	1	³⁄₁₆ x 12 x 18 inches (5 x 300 x 460 mm)
Suggested lumber		A and B – Ash
		C – Elm
		D – Ash-faced plywood
Suggested finish		Danish oil, clear polyurethane varnish, wax or black- or white-colored satin lacquer
Alternative lumber		A hardwood such as oak or beech
Notes		
*Both handles are cut from the same piece of lumber		

Above *A corner dovetail joint. The finish darkens the grain and accentuates the visual effect*

End view

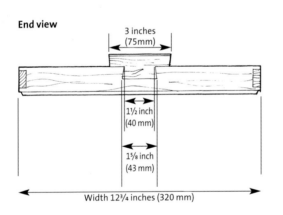

3 inches (75mm)

1½ inch (40 mm)

1⁵⁄₈ inch (43 mm)

Width 12¾ inches (320 mm)

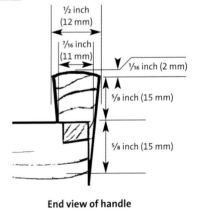

½ inch (12 mm)

⁷⁄₁₆ inch (11 mm)

¹⁄₁₆ inch (2 mm)

⁵⁄₈ inch (15 mm)

⁵⁄₈ inch (15 mm)

End view of handle

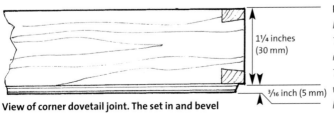

1¼ inches (30 mm)

³⁄₁₆ inch (5 mm)

View of corner dovetail joint. The set in and bevel of the bottom are clearly shown.

Notes
Not to scale.
The types of wood chosen make a big difference. Thoughtful balancing of the woods selected for the frame, handles and base will create a pleasing effect.

Above *Breakfast tray made in ash and elm with dovetail joints at its corners and handles*

Right *The handles, tapered from top to bottom, provide a positive grip and subtle visual detail*

Far right *The base of the tray is beveled and set back slightly from the edges of the sides*

Construction

TOOLS & EQUIPMENT

Cutting gauge

Sliding bevel

Pencil

Small try square

Dovetail saw

Small marking knife

C-clamps

Bevel-edged chisel: ½ inch
(12 mm)

Smoothing plane

Sanding block

Waterproof glue and brush

Two sash clamps

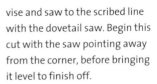

MARKING AND CUTTING THE DOVETAILS

1 Mark out and cut the four dovetails at the ends of the side pieces, following the sequence described on pages 31–32. (The tray's corner joints are simpler than those made previously but the process is identical except that only one joint is required instead of three.)

To remove the outside waste, clamp the work vertically in the vise and saw to the scribed line with the dovetail saw. Begin this cut with the saw pointing away from the corner, before bringing it level to finish off.

MARKING AND CUTTING THE PINS

2 The accurate marking of the pins, which in this case fall only at either side of the dovetail, is one of the secrets of a neat dovetail joint. This is done by scribing the pins directly off the corresponding dovetail part of the joint. Since the space is confined, a small knife is easier to use than the usual marking knife. Fill in the scribed lines with a sharp pencil at once as they can be difficult to see.

3 Clamp the work vertically in the vise before cutting the pins. Make some initial strokes with the saw held vertically before changing the angle to follow the scribed lines. This reduces the tendency of the saw to follow the grain of the wood rather than the cutting line.

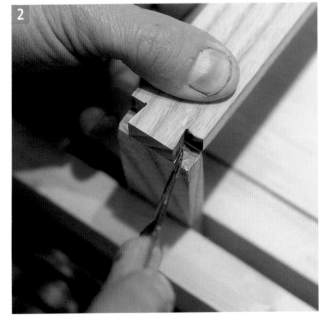

4 Check the fit by fitting the dovetails with the pins. Mark the adjacent corners AA, BB, CC, DD. This is important because the pins for each joint have been individually scribed and fitted.

THE HANDLES

5 Begin by marking the lengths of both handles; then mark centerlines along the length and width. The handle dovetails can then be marked out. The handle stock is left in one piece for the time being, since the longer piece of wood is easier to work on than two small blocks.

6 Now saw the two handle dovetails following the instructions in Step 1.

7 Finally, chisel out the waste around the handles. Push down gently on the chisel by hand, holding it perpendicular to the joint to ensure a clean finish.

8 Pare the sides of the dovetails flat and clean with a bevel-edged chisel. Accurate cleaning of these surfaces will make fitting easier later on.

9 To taper each side of the handles slightly, hold each handle in the vise and smooth it with a plane.

10 Mark the holes for the handles in the ends of the tray in a similar way to the pins in the corner joints (see Step 2).

Remove the waste following the procedure for the corner pins. You will find it best to cut the waste to just short of the centerline; then pare it back with the chisel until a tight push fit is achieved.

11 Round the tops of the handles using either a plane or a sanding block for a neat finish and a smooth feel.

THE BASE

12 Trim the plywood for the base to ⅛ inch (3 mm) less than the size of the tray frame all the way round. Using a plane, bevel the edge of the base to 45° so that it will not be visible when the tray is sitting on a table.

ASSEMBLY

13 Fit the handles first. (A waterproof wood glue is essential as the tray will come into contact with water.) Apply glue to the ends of the tray that will be in contact with the handles; then push each handle into position. Leave it to dry; then clean up the excess glue with a sharp chisel.

Next apply glue to all the mating surfaces of the corner joints. Clamp the joints with sash clamps. Clean up the inside of each joint with a chisel and the outside with the smoothing plane. Carefully sand the frame with a sanding block before fitting the base.

With the tray upside down, apply glue to the frame and base mating surfaces. Put the base in place and weight it down until the glue has set. Scrape off any excess glue with a sharp chisel.

FINISHING

14 The finish protects the wood from inevitable spillages and allows the tray to be wiped over after use. The finish also brings out the color in the wood, which will highlight the contrast between the different types of wood used for the tray frame and the handles.

The finish needs to be water-resistant (such as polyurethane), built up in two to three thinned coats. This may then be burnished with wire wool and polished with finishing wax.

Tool section

THE HAND TOOLS and small machine tools in this directory used for woodworking are those most commonly found in the small workshop. Whenever buying tools, especially hand tools, always buy the very best you can afford. A good hand tool will last more than one lifetime and quite often second-hand tools offer very good value for money. Buy hand tools as you need them rather than because you feel you should have them. Many professional craftspeople own a relatively small selection of tools but use all of them to great effect.

Measuring and marking tools

Steel tape measure
This is used for rough measuring and marking. Do not use it for accurate work.

Imperial/metric steel rule
The primary tool for accurate measuring in the workshop.

Combination square
Spend a lot of money on a high-quality set and you will be repaid with accurate measurements of squares and angles.

Cutting gauge
A rosewood marking gauge with a knurled brass adjusting knob.

Dovetail squares
Two gauges for marking up dovetails in hardwood (1:8) and softwood (1:6), respectively.

Marking gauge
A conventional pattern, single-stem marking gauge widely used with a plastic adjustment screw.

Beveled straightedge
A good straightedge is invaluable for checking the flatness of surfaces.

Sliding bevel
Shown here with a wooden handle. The bevel is set from a protractor.

Rosewood mortise gauge
Fitted here with a very precise brass adjusting mechanism, which makes this a very reliable and useful tool.

Dovetail markers
These are used for marking out dovetails quickly and accurately.

Dividers
These are fitted with a spring joint for precise settings.

Engineer's square
An all-steel engineer's square is far more accurate than one with a wooden stock.

Engineer's sliding bevel
An all-steel version of the above tool. Both are used for measuring and marking out angles.

English pattern marking knife
Widely available but frequently supplied with an inferior-quality steel blade.

Digital readout calipers
Used for measuring and checking the thickness of components.

Carpenter's square
Used for site work and less accurate work than the all-steel engineer's square.

Miter square
A 45° square, used for marking out mitres.

Japanese marking knife
High-quality laminated steel makes this a very useful piece of equipment.

Spirit level
A traditional teak level with a brass top plate.

Saws

Panel saw
The shortest of the bench saws used for small-scale joinery work.

Crosscut saw
A slightly longer saw used in solid hardwood and sheet material.

Ripsaw
Mostly used for ripping solid wood down the grain.

Dovetail saw
8 or 10 inches (200 or 250 mm) in length, used for small joinery work.

Tenon saw
Usually 12 inches in length, used for larger-scale joinery work.

Gent's saw
Occasionally called a jeweler's saw, this is used for small-scale joinery work.

Coping saw
Designed to make curved cuts in wood.

Adjustable piercing saw
The piercing saw or jeweller's bowsaw is used for extremely fine work.

Jigsaw
A hand-held power tool used for curved work.

Miter trimmer
Small saw used for trimming end grain on components.

Miter saw
A small machine that helps cut more accurate miters.

Band saw
A small and useful machine used for cutting curves and straight components.

Biscuit joiner
Used for very quick joinery processes.

Circular saw
Shown here as a cordless version of the popular hand-held circular saw.

Table saw
Small bench-mounted machine comprising a circular saw fitted in a machine table.

Router

Plunge router
Shown here with variable speed. This is a large heavy-duty router.

Planing and shaping tools

Smoothing planes
Available in wood and metal, these are used for final finishing of already flat surfaces.

Side rabbet plane
Used occasionally for enlarging the width of a groove or rabbet.

Block planes
Small and very useful bench planes frequently used on end grain.

Edge trimming plane
A specialist plane used to plane an edge at 90° to an existing surface.

Jack planes
These are general-purpose bench planes used in every cabinetmaking workshop.

Small shoulder plane
Used for very delicate work.

Compass plane
Used for planing curved surfaces.

Medium-sized shoulder plane
Useful for general-purpose trimming and small joinery work.

Jointer planes
Long-soled bench planes, occasionally used for surfacing edges on boards.

Combination shoulder plane
A versatile tool that can be used as a shoulder, rabbet or chisel plane.

Cabinet scrapers
Used for finishing surfaces.

Spokeshave
A widely used hand-held shaping tool.

Scraper plane
Used for scraping flat surfaces.

Cabinet rasp
Used for filing and shaping curved surfaces.

Power plane
A hand-held power plane used for planing narrow components.

Planer/thicknesser
Used for both planing and thicknessing material.

Chisels

Bevel-edged chisel
A general-purpose and widely used bench chisel.

Large mortise chisel
A heavy-patterned chisel, with a leather washer and steel ferrule on the top of the handle, for use with a heavy mallet.

Small firmer chisel
Similar to the above, but with a lighter handle and not used for heavy mallet work.

Japanese chisels
Exceptional high-quality but heavy-patterned bevel-edged chisels.

Paring chisel
A long-bladed bevel-edged chisel used for delicate paring work.

Cranked paring chisel
A paring chisel with a cranked handle enabling it to reach inside carcasses more easily.

Right- and left-handed skew chisels
The slicing action of these sharp-pointed, bevel-edged chisels is useful for finishing joints.

Drilling and mortising tools

Carpenter's brace
Used with lip-and-spur (Jennings) pattern bits for boring holes in wood by hand.

Drill stand
Small stand used to turn an electric drill into a bench machine.

Wheel brace
Small hand-held brace

Cordless electric drill
Widely used for drilling, sanding and shaping.

Mortising machine
Used to drill square holes for mortises.

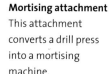

Mortising attachment
This attachment converts a drill press into a mortising machine.

Dust extractors

Bench drill press
Popular for drilling accurate 90° holes in components.

Floor-mounted drill press
The floor-standing version of the bench drill does not take up valuable bench space.

Single-bag dust extractor
Used to keep the workshop free of dust and shavings, this is essential when machining.

Small extractor
This can be attached to power tools or used to clean around the bench. It is shown here attached to a router.

Clamps and assembly tools

C-clamp
Capable of applying considerable pressure during assembly to bring components together.

Board clamps
A panel clamping system that does a similar job to the sash clamp.

Deep-throat clamp
Similar to the above but with a bigger reach.

Aluminium sash clamp
A light, strong and accurate clamp, useful for small work.

Band or strap clamp
Used here to assemble a light frame.

Fast-acting clamp
Similar to the above but faster to set up and fix on the job during assembly.

Supports

Lightweight sash clamp
Used for assembly of large flat components.

Cabinetmaker's bench
Shown here with an end vise and a tail vise. This is the most important tool in the workshop.

Machine table
This accepts jigsaws, routers and circular saws and converts each of them into a stationary machine.

T-bar sash clamp
Expensive but widely used in professional workshops for assembling large components.

Bar clamp
Versatile clamp that applies pressure both inward and outward if heads are reversed.

Saw horse
Usually workshop made, trestles are very useful supports for half-completed work and components.

Bench hook
Used for holding small components while sawing them to size.

This book first appeared as part of *The Hamlyn Book of Woodworking*

First published in Great Britain in this form in 2001 by Hamlyn, an imprint of Octopus Publishing Group Ltd
2–4 Heron Quays, London E14 4JP

Copyright © Octopus Publishing Group Ltd 2001

ISBN 0 600 60301 6

A CIP catalogue record for this book is available from the British Library

Printed and bound in China

In describing all the woodworking practices and projects in this book, every care has been taken to recommend the safest methods of working. Before starting any task, you should be confident that you know what you are doing, and that you know how to use all tools and equipment safely. The Publishers cannot accept any legal responsibility or liability for any direct or consequential accidents or damage arising from the use of any items mentioned, or in the carrying out of any of the projects described.

Contents

oints and
ointmakin

Professional
skills made easy

hamlyn